Absolute C

Pirates of Somalia

The Hijacking and Daring Rescue of MV Maersk Alabama

ABSOLUTE CRIME

By John Fleury

Absolute Crime Books

www.absolutecrime.com

Cover Image © il-fede - Fotolia.com

Table of Contents

About Us

Absolute Crime publishes only the best true crime literature. Our focus is on the crimes that you've probably never heard of, but you are fascinated to read more about. With each engaging and gripping story, we try to let readers relive moments in history that some people have tried to forget.

Remember, our books are not meant for the faint at heart. We don't hold back — if a crime is bloody, we let the words splatter across the page so you can experience the crime in the most horrifying way!

If you enjoy this book, please visit our homepage to see other books we offer; if you have any feedback, we'd love to hear from you!

Prologue

Captain Richard Phillips stood before his ship, the Maersk Alabama. It was Wednesday, April 8, 2009. The day was early. The sun was just coming up, warming the small country of Djibouti. The captain inspected the American cargo vessel that he was in charge of. He heard the voices of his crew who had just climbed aboard. Laughter. Camaraderie. Unsuspecting. The captain's mind wondered back to the messages he'd received from maritime safety groups in the days that led up to this one. Their messages were warnings. Each featured the same key word: Pirates. Captain Phillips took a deep breath through his nostrils, sucking in the fresh morning air. He released the breath of air from his mouth and climbed aboard the ship.

Chapter 1: Set Sail, Hark Back

The morning was unfolding, slowly brightening the further the Maersk Alabama sailed. They were headed for Mombasa in Kenya. The captain and his crew's mission was to deliver 17,000 tonnes of cargo that included UN food aid for the starving peoples of Africa. The crew was busy but Captain Phillips' mind was still distracted by that one word: pirates. Like a fish that had taken the bait his mind was unable to let go of it.

What did he know of pirates? the captain wondered to himself. He was aware of modern piracy. He'd seen the news. Seen the bandits clad in rags. Seen the AK-47s in the grip of their hands. Seen the mixed look of vexation and desperation in their eyes. Yet that very word 'pirate' conjured up stereotypical cartoonish images of men of the sea dressed in waistcoats and eye-patches and bandanas and brandishing cutlasses, led by a rum-swigging captain with a wooden leg, a flamboyant attire and a parrot on his shoulder.

The captain's mind was taken on a journey back down memory lane where characters from his childhood still lurked, such as Blackbeard and Henry Morgan, and fictional representatives like *Treasure Island's* Long John Silver and even Disney's *Peter Pan* villain, Captain Hook. From so early on the legend of pirates had been romanticised by these variants. But Captain Phillips was an educated man. He knew what piracy's origins really beheld.

The captain knew the very word 'pirates' wasn't the charming stuff of kids tales, but more like the Frankish and Saxon gangs of the sea who had ruthlessly plagued the waters of Armorica and Belgic Gaul in 286 AD. To rid them of their nuisance a hero was introduced in the form of Carausius – a Roman military commander who began life in simple circumstances but rose to power with his leadership and bravery. Taking reign of the Classis Britannica he entered battle on the waters, conquered the pirates and eliminated their threat.

Captain Phillips continued to steer the ship towards its final destination while his mind played out a history lesson from the depths of his learning. Like an opened treasure chest rich information poured out. The first known documented recording of official piracy was extracted and it dated back to the 14th century. On this document was stated the pirates in question of this era – the Sea Peoples who tormented southern Europe – the areas around the Aegean Sea in particular – and the eastern Mediterranean. Anatolia, Syria, Canaan, Cyprus and Egypt all came under invasion, a narrator read aloud from the document.

The captain's eyes were fixed on the waters of the Indian Ocean ahead but upon them played out the most prominent period of piracy, which came between the Middle Ages and the 19th century. The waters had begun flourishing with commerce, setting forth the path that Captain Phillips and his men and the modern-day pirates would inherit.

A fast-forwarded montage skipped across the waters in front of the captain. During the extensive period between the Middle Ages and the 19th century tales had begun to emerge all around the world: East Asian pirates had started hijacking the silk and spice routes and preying on the junk trade of China; the notorious Vikings were savage warriors who commanded western Europe between the 8th and 12th centuries through their daring and violent raids; North Africa became known as the 'Barbary Coast' due to the looting carried out by the Barbary corsairs; and in North America during this period the legendary Blackbeard dominated the coasts, callously attacking ships that dared cross his path.

It was the Caribbean in particular, however, that experienced the greatest era of piracy with an extensive period that began around 1560 and lasted until the mid-1720s.

Captain Phillips' fast-forwarded montage slowed down as attacks carried out on Spanish ships by the buccaneers and the domination of British-born Henry Morgan played out. Piracy in the Caribbean was rife due to the control Spain had of the islands, the history narrator reminded the captain. As a result of the rivalry European pirates from Britain, Portugal, France and the Netherlands often fought and raided the cargo ships that were occupied by the Spanish pirates.

His crewmen brought Captain Phillips' attention back to the present. They were 400 miles east of Somalia's capital, Mogadishu. The captain's heart is strangled for a moment by the reminder of the word that has haunted him for days – pirates. As prevalent as piracy was in the past it never died out. Somali pirates now carried the flag of threat on the seas. And their stomping ground was the area in the Horn of Africa in which the Maersk Alabama was now dangerously headed into.

Chapter 2: A Country at War With Itself

As the ship cut through the sloshing waters Captain Phillips' eyes scanned for invaders. The morning was crisp. Cool. He tried to apply the same to his nerves. The crew was trained. They had been prepared for an attack. The men set into motion. As his eyes squinted behind his spectacles Captain Phillips' active mind betrayed him once again. Like an internet search engine it fed in the words 'pirates' and 'Somalia' and relayed the information it had like a newsreel.

The year was 1991. The country of Somalia had entered civil war. The military government had been usurped by opposition groups. The war had never ceased. It raged on and with it spurned hatred among its once peaceful people. The citizens were fed up. They were angered. They were desperate.

Fast forward. The year was 2005. News reports began to emerge of pirates operating off the coast of the warring country. Reasons of how this was conceived were flung from one side to the other like a tennis game. Illegal fishing, yelled the United Nations. Toxic waste, screamed the U.S. House Armed Services Committee. Noble heroes, whispered the locals of Somalia

With a shake of his head Captain Phillips wondered if more could have been done for them. The delay in action had prolonged the threat upon the waters of the Arabian Sea and the Indian Ocean. And the result had come at a huge cost, between $6.6 and $6.9 billion every year to be precise. That's what it boiled down to, thought the captain. While the Somali people have nothing the rest of the world increased shipping expenses to whopping sums of money. No wonder they were so bitter against the world.

Captain Phillips recalled an incident back in May 2007. Somali pirates off the coast of their land spotted a Taiwanese fishing ship called the Ching Fong Hwa No. 168. The ship had 14 crewmen aboard. Every one of them was taken hostage. Every one of them was kept hostage until November. One of them did not make it out alive.

The Somali pirates were frustrated, angered, embittered at not being taken seriously. They wanted a ransom to be paid. Yet they received nothing. So they took a crewman's life instead and released the ship, along with its corpse and mentally scarred crew and captain, to Mombasa, Kenya – the same destination where the Maersk Alabama was headed for.

Captain Phillips looked at his crewmen and a cold shiver ran up his spine. He looked at his hands and a fear swept over him as he imagined them stained with the blood of his colleagues. Just like the captain of that Taiwanese fishing ship whose hands were forever marked. The captain averted his gaze to the heavens. But God wasn't there. Only cold statistics that frenzied his anxious mind.

A year after the attack on the Taiwanese ship a further 111 attacks were carried out. Forty-two were successful. Captain Phillips shut his eyes in an effort to block the terrifying information. A resolution's been set up, the soothing voice of his conscience reassured him. Military force could be taken should the ship come under attack. Then why was the Maersk Alabama unarmed? This question alarmed the captain. A trigger had been pulled and more harrowing questions were released into the whirlpool of his mind. If the resolution had been created in October 2008 then why, just a month later, had the pirates felt bold enough to expand their terror to the Gulf of Aden? Why had they not been deterred? Why, at the turn of the year, had the months of January and February incurred ten times more attacks than the same period the previous year? Why had there been near daily attacks throughout March? Seventy-nine attacks this year, hissed a tormented voice in the shaken captain's ears.

Captain Phillips trembled. His eyes opened. Tears had crept to their surface. Another question came to his mind: What have I done?

Chapter 3: The Maersk Alabama

Captain Phillips composed himself. He couldn't allow his men to see him looking so troubled. He was their leader. They looked up to him. He threw the thoughts that had plagued him overboard. He dictated some orders to his men with the compassion and steely leadership they expected of him. They had each grown an admiration for Captain Phillips. He was a good captain. A good man. A good friend.

The captain summoned Chief Engineer Mike Perry, an athletically built and youthful-looking man despite his 61 years of age. The captain knew he could trust Chief Engineer Perry for he saw qualities of leadership within him, too. He used that word that hissed in his ears – pirates. Chief Engineer Perry didn't flinch. He was a strong man with nerves encased in marble. He nodded to the captain and took his position on the deck to keep watch.

The captain, watching Chief Engineer Perry walk away, nodded to himself. He was glad to have a man like him by his side. They had worked together on the Maersk Alabama for many years.

The Maersk Alabama…the words were enough to carve a smile through the captain's beard. His ship had a special place in his heart. Of course it was known as the Alva Maersk when it was born in 1994. Built by the Chinese and flagged to Denmark it remained in Scandinavia for four years until it was reflagged to Norfolk, Virginia in the USA. That transitional period wasn't as joyous as it should have been though. The smile slipped away as the captain remembered the event that had been described to him once before.

October 1 2004. A proud announcement was made by Maersk Line Ltd (MLL). An agreement had been signed with the Maritime Administration that would see the transfer of six Maritime Security Program (MSP) modern containerships. They were to replace the six vessels that were currently used. The six vessels that were being used were badly out of date, having been built in the 1980s. One of the new containerships was the Alva Maersk.

As the Alva Maersk arrived in Dubai on November 10 the company appeared to be going from strength-to-strength with yet another announcement of their base relocating to the United States of America and their name changing to Maersk Alabama.

The company was excited by the succession of these six new containerships. They would become a huge asset to the U.S.'s flag-fleet operations, while the MLL's global network would expand with their introduction. With this it seemed company and country would benefit immensely from the new vessels. But the gloss of this new varnish would soon wear off when bogus shipping contracts were exposed and the Maersk Alabama was detained in Kuwait.

The Danish liner company claimed that Kuwait-based Indian nationals were behind the scam, including the entrepreneurial Arwen Singh Sahni and his family and associates. By May 2005 Maersk were in US courts clutching papers that they had filed with the Southern District of New York federal court and chasing treble damages worth $24.95m. The case against Singh Sahni and co was that low-value goods had been shipped under the false pretence that they were actually goods on high-value bills of lading, and then suing Maersk for the loss of merchandise that never actually existed. The Maersk Alabama's involvement in the whole scheme came about when the alleged fraudsters succeeded in getting the ship arrested and detained in Kuwait as collateral. In order to retrieve the ship Maersk had to pay out $1.86m.

It was a dark cloud that had hung over the ship since, thought Captain Phillips. What the captain didn't know was that a fierce storm was brewing within that cloud.

Chapter 4: The Hijacking

When the crew noticed Chief Engineer Perry on the deck they knew instantly what to do. Each man was set in motion, prepared for the potential. They were trained. They had been trained in union schools in anti-piracy. It was only the day before that they had carried out a safety drill aboard their ship, led by second in command Captain Shane Murphy, son of an instructor at the Massachusetts Maritime Academy who specialised in courses that teach how to prevent pirate attacks. The men knew just how dangerous the waters were.

It was only a few days back, on the weekend, when a French yacht was captured by gun-wielding pirates, as was a Yemeni tug boat and a 20,000-tonne German container vessel, known as Hansa Stavanger.

The Hansa Stavanger had a crew that consisted of a German captain, three Russians, two Ukrainians and 14 Filipinos. That's a crew of 20 men. The same total as the men on the Maersk Alabama. The Somali pirates had been unperturbed by being outnumbered. The way they saw it, this was their territory, which meant anything to enter that was also theirs. And they would be willing to take it by any means necessary.

These stories were exchanged between the men through hushed whispers. The year before the pirates had succeeded with the audacious hijackings of a Saudi supertanker, explained one veteran. It called the Sirius Star. It was transporting $100 million worth of crude oil. The same applied to a Ukrainian cargo ship that was loaded with heavy weaponry, including 33 Soviet-era T-72 tanks, responded another veteran crewman. The rest of the crew learned how under the control of the pirates the seized ships were transported to remote coastal village bases in Somalia where they were kept until a ransom was paid out. If the ransom could be paid out, that is. For the kidnapped crew members who had become hostages their lives were gratefully spared. In January the 25 crewmen of the Sirius Star were freed after a $3 million ransom was parachuted onto its deck, which the Somali pirates hungrily stole away. Again in February the crew and Ukrainian ship were released after payment was successfully made to the pirates. The ransom this time had increased to $3.2 million.

Meanwhile, back on the deck Chief Engineer Mike Perry looked out across the dark waters. Some time passed. He could hear the crewmen behind him, busying themselves for what may occur. The morning air was crisp. The smell of the sea filled his nostrils. It refreshed his lungs. Not too far out he could see the Somali coast. While his eyes trained on the geography of the African land something else suddenly came into his view. He grabbed a pair of binoculars. Fixed his gaze once more. Pulled away from what he saw. At first he wasn't sure. Now, he knew for certain. Much as he had anticipated, pirates were headed their way.

They were armed to the teeth with AK-47s and pistols. He saw four of them in total aboard the FV Win Far 161. He recognised it as a Taiwanese fishing vessel that had been captured just days before on the waters near the Seychelles. Perry saw the determination and drive etched on the faces of the men approaching them. A look at his watch told him it was 7:15 in the morning. He was left with no choice but to alert his colleagues of the oncoming situation. The hearts of the men froze when Chief Engineer Perry told them the information. But they were not frozen for long. The fire of their loyalty ignited them into action. The 500-foot Maersk Alabama came alive with their controlled workmanship like an ant kingdom.

Doors to the engine room were secured. Then, under the calmness of Captain Phillips, 14 of the crewmen, some of whom were grandfathers, made their way to the secure room, which the engineers had fortified for such an occasion. As the 15 men made their way the captain demonstrated his leadership qualities. Not one of them was aware that his heart beat against the barrier of his chest with the anxiety of a cornered animal.

Back on deck some of the men fired flares into the heavens in an effort to notify other ships in their proximity that their vessel was expecting an attack. As the flares burst into colours above them Chief Engineer Perry and First Officer Matt Fisher attempted to thwart the pirates by swinging the ship's rudder and swamping the pirate skiff. They succeeded in overturning the skiff, but the pirates were not defeated. The defensive efforts of the Americans were in vain.

The pirates each grabbed hold of the ropes that were hanging from the side of the ship and began their ascension. There was nothing Perry and his men could do except prepare themselves for combat on board. As the pirates clambered over they fired shots into the air – a signal that they had intruded and a warning to the crewmen. As they quickly made their way to the bridge a crewman by the name of Reza sounded the alarm. Seconds later, he had a gun pointed to his face.

Chief Engineer Perry assumed control of the ship's propulsion and steering. The remaining crew rushed for the safety of the secure room. When his comrades had all crammed inside Chief Engineer Perry was left with no choice but to turn off all the ventilation and lights on board the Maersk Alabama so the pirates could not assume control. Blanketed in darkness and with the heat rising little did any of the men know that Reza was now in the hands of the pirates.

Understanding the ship better than the intruders Chief Engineer Perry, equipped with a knife, quietly and methodically made his way through the darkness to the secure room. Once outside, he assumed his position and lay in wait, silently and calmly expecting the pirates any minute and preparing himself to fight them to the death in protection of the lives of the men he worked with.

#   #   #

Hours passed and the crew began to grow dehydrated; the temperature had risen to as high as 130 degrees. Pouring with sweat and with only a rusted bucket of dirty water to share between them they were left helpless in the suspense.

Then, all of a sudden and out of nowhere, they heard angry shouts in broken English coming from the distance. The shouts were directed at the men. The shouts were coming from the pirates. The shouts were telling them that they had Reza and were prepared to kill him. The men, including Chief Engineer Perry, remained silent and prayed for the life of their colleague.

And then a shot was fired and the explosion of the sound erupted in violent echoes around them.

Reza was assumed dead and the men began to mourn for their fallen crew member. The sign of the cross was made numerous times in the darkness. But Reza was very much alive. The pirates had fired the shot in an effort to lure the men out of hiding. Sensing that he needed to do something in order to protect the lives of his band of brothers, Reza began to devise a plan.

Still on the bridge where they had taken him hostage Reza began to negotiate with the pirates by volunteering to take one of them to the engine room so they could assume control of the ship. To his amazement, they agreed and the leader of the gang offered to follow Reza. Further to Reza's amazement, the leader even decided to leave his gun behind with his men on account that he may not be able to return with more hostages if he was armed because they may be too afraid to cooperate. And so, Reza led the way into the darkness of the ship's interior, closely pursued by the trusting pirate leader.

Chief Engineer Perry heard the approach of the two men's footsteps and like a predator in the jungle he steadied himself for the attack upon his prey. Moments later they were before him and without warning he leaped from his spot towards the figures. Reza and Perry began grappling with the pirate as they tackled him to the ground. Hearing the commotion right outside the door several of the crewmen burst out to assist their colleagues. Outnumbered and overpowered the pirate was pinned down to the ground, had his hands tied together with wire, and then taken captive. During the melee, however, he was wounded. His left hand had been opened up by the blade in Chief Engineer Perry's own hand, and he was suffering heavy blood loss.

With the band leader injured and under their control the crew of the Maersk Alabama found themselves in a position of power. Expecting the pirates to come looking for their leader, but not wanting to get themselves into a battle that they could not possibly win being as the ship was unarmed, the men sat in wait with their hostage.

\#   \#   \#

It had been 12 hours since the pirates had hijacked the ship before the crew eventually decided that they had to go back out to the bridge and confront the men. With their hostage in tow all the men made their way back to the bridge. Assuming control of the pirate the crew frog-marched him to the other pirates, and soon they came face-to-face with the remainder of the gang. Upon seeing their leader taken hostage with his badly damaged hand the angered pirates lifted their guns, simultaneously clicked off the safety catch and prepared to open fire.

In the seconds of ensuing panic and fearing more bloodshed Captain Phillips knew he had to do something. So he stepped forward. The manic pirates immediately turned their attention, and their guns, to him. They screamed at him to get back or they would shoot. To defuse the situation Captain Phillips calmly and silently raised his hands. His open palms faced them as an indicator to the villains that he meant no threat.

With the entire ship's attention and convinced the pirates would not fire at him, the captain volunteered himself as their hostage in order to safeguard his men. Not waiting for their response Captain Phillips walked towards them resolutely. In the secure room the captain had had a calming effect over his crew amid the increasing uncertainty over their fate. And so it was again that he provided reassurance to his men. Accepting the Maersk Alabama's leader in exchange for their own the pirates made more demands. In order to safely exchange hostages they wanted to make their getaway with the provision of a boat, fuel and food.

The crew accepted the terms. Fuel and food were brought forward. They were stored inside an orange lifeboat, which was handed over to the pirates. Settling into their newly acquired boat the pirates demanded the release of their leader. The crew willingly allowed their hostage to go free. Once he was reacquainted with his men, clutching his badly wounded hand, the crew requested the freedom of Captain Phillips.

Staring into the eyes of the men aboard the ship the pirates refused point blank and smiled ruthlessly as they manoeuvred the lifeboat away from its mother ship. They may not have gotten away with the entire ship as they had set out to do, but with the captain of the Maersk Alabama the pirates knew they could hold the Americans to ransom. The crew could do nothing but watch hopelessly on. Their brave captain's life was now in the hands of the bandits of the Indian Ocean.

Fifteen hours after the pirates had invaded their morning.

Their ship.

Their lives.

Chapter 5: The Reaction of the World

The lifeboat sailed away from the Maersk Alabama. Chief Engineer Perry and the other men watched on furiously, helpless in preventing it. Some of the crew tore themselves away from the scene. They were finally able to radio in to their base. Shortly after doing so the hijacking had become worldwide news.

Reporters described the ordeal to disbelieving viewers. The public was fed information that left them stunned: in only the four months of that year there had been more than 60 attacks carried out by pirates off the coast of Somalia. Sixteen ships remained under their control. Negotiations remained on-going with their owners over ransom fees.

The world learned how this attack had been the first to be carried out on an American vessel. Worst of all, though, the global media was disgusted and outraged by the ruthlessness of the pirates. How could they be so callous as to attack a vessel that was transporting food aid for the World Food Program, a United Nations agency? How could they be so treacherous in going against the agreement they had made with the crew in the exchange of hostages? How could they, indeed, take the captain as their captive when he had bravely stepped forward to save the life of his men? How did the pirates have the audacity to attack an American vessel that was within a region that had lately become patrolled by American warships? How would the new American government under President Obama respond to this atrocity?

There were no answers to these questions. But what the media and public did have was high praise for the crew in the way they handled the attack. Though the crew was forced to turn off the ship's system, which meant an alert could not be sent out earlier, the media and the government were in agreement that this was the correct decision as it ensured that the entire ship's crew was not taken hostage, which they would have been had the pirates succeeded in taking control of the ship. For this reason, Chief Engineer Perry received particular praise, as did his colleagues Fisher and Reza for the roles they played. Essential praise was made to the captured Captain Phillips however, who was deemed a hero for volunteering himself as a hostage to the pirates.

While the media and the public discussed the hot topic the US Navy and the government got down to devising a rescue plan. The Navy hardly ever engaged with pirates because of the risk posed to hostages. This had been enforced by the American government. They had learned from the French government's hot-headed retaliation to a French yacht that had been hijacked by Somali pirates. With guns blazing the French had succeeded in freeing four of the hostages, including one child. But their freedom had come at the cost of the execution of two pirates – and tragically, a fifth hostage. The Americans did not want to take the same risk.

In previous occasions where cargo was deemed precious, such as weaponry, the US warships had encircled the hijacked ship so the route was blocked. This prevented the cargo from reaching the mainland. This peaceful measure had previously proven successful. However, the circumstances surrounding the Maersk Alabama had changed matters. The Americans were forced into rethinking their operations. Paying a ransom was not an option because that would mean the pirates had won.

Captain Phillips. The Maersk Alabama crew. Bravery. These select words held a special amount of strength to the Navy and the government. They knew they had to do whatever it took to rescue the captive captain. While the government thought about how best to hatch the egg of their plan, the destroyer USS Bainbridge made its way to the Maersk Alabama after being alerted to the situation. They reached the ship early on April 9.

After the Maersk Alabama was reached by the guided-missile destroyer – led by Navy Commander Frank Castellano, a man with a kind face but an unbreakable nerve – it and the crew was escorted to its original destination of Mombasa, Kenya.

With the Maersk Alabama in safety Commander Castellano led the Bainbridge into the night. Under the cover of darkness the Bainbridge was able to locate the orange lifeboat. With it in their sight Commander Castellano ordered for them to maintain a cautionary distance. He did not want to scare the pirates into opening fire.

The rescue team on the American destroyer plotted their next careful move in the mission that was being monitored by the whole world.

Chapter 6: The Rescue

Sixty-two hours passed by with the American destroyer monitoring the pirates' every movement. In that time Commander Castellano and some of the Navy aboard the Bainbridge had seen Captain Phillips attempt an escape. Through night-vision goggles they witnessed the green body of the captain dive from the lifeboat into the black waters of the Indian Ocean. While he frantically swam away from the boat one of the pirates dived in after him. Another one of the pirates on the lifeboat grabbed hold of his AK-47. Without warning the disturbing sound of rapid shots disrupted the night. The bullets hit the water around the captain with extreme ferocity. Commander Castellano realised that the pirate was deliberately aiming away from the captain. The commander knew why he was doing this. He wanted to frighten the captain into slowing down. The captain, however, thought the pirate was trying to kill him. He being dead though would be no use to them. They needed him alive because his life, to them, was worth millions of dollars. The commander knew this, too, which is why he prevented any action being taken by the Navy.

The dastardly plan worked. Moments later the captain, like a chased prey suffering fatigue and fear, began to slow down. A third pirate emerged on the boat. He saw the captain slow down. Seconds later, his green figure was submerged in the water. The captain had two predators coming for him.

It was with ease that together they caught the captain and hauled him back to the lifeboat. Under Commander Castellano's orders the Bainbridge still didn't move or attempt to intervene. He knew that doing so would potentially lead to the captain's execution. There was no way he was going to allow the blood on his hands. Without realising it the commander had had the exact same thought as the captain had.

This occurrence took place on Thursday night. That morning Commander Castellano had communicated with the pirates for the first time. Tuning into a walkie-talkie that they'd stolen from the Maersk Alabama Commander Castellano listened patiently to the demands they made. They wanted a clear and safe passage to Somalia. They promised that once they reached the shore they would release their hostage. Commander Castellano knew full well how hollow their promises were. If their demands were not met, the pirates were willing to die at sea, and the captain would die with them.

The morning after the captain's attempted escape the pirates refused to allow Commander Castellano and his crew to communicate with Captain Phillips. From the deck of their ship the Bainbridge crew eventually managed to spot the captain inside the lifeboat. His hands had been bound behind his back. After that, reinforcements were called in. Soon, the USS Bainbridge was joined by two more warships – the USS Halyburton and the USS Boxer.

#   #   #

By Saturday, the pirates' attitudes were fluctuating, which Commander Castellano put down to their lack of sleep and basic comforts such as a toilet and ventilation. Later in the day, the pirates had endured enough and decided to hit back. Putting their lifeboat into action they accelerated towards the Somali coast.

The Navy's intentions were to prevent them from reaching the mainland. The pirates were fully aware of this, but they were not going to go down without trying. One of the tactics adopted by the Navy was to use powerful fire hoses to redirect the course of the lifeboat in an effort to tire out the gang on board and force them into submission. Time and time again the force of the water slammed into the small craft pushing it away from its intended route. The pirates were warriors of the sea though, and they were not willing to submit so easily.

Conceding that the fire hose was not enough the Navy decided to pull out another tool from their heavy arsenal – a seahawk helicopter. The airborne beast hovered directly above the lifeboat. This method generated hurricane-force winds from the extremely powerful rotors. Rocked back in the winds the pirates were thrown to the ground clutching their ears in an effort to block out the extremely loud and aggressive sounds of the helicopter that reverberated around the claustrophobic confinement of the tiny lifeboat. The pirates' will was being tested and the Navy expected them to drop down their weapons and give themselves up at any time.

Pushed further and further away from the mainland the pirates exchanged knowing looks with one another. They had no idea what would happen next. Perhaps some of the Navy would jump down from the helicopter and take the lifeboat by force? Panic was reflected back at the men from the eyes of their fellow gang members. Sensing that they were beginning to wear down the resilience of the pirates the Navy opted to take it yet another step further.

With the other warships enforcing the USS Bainbridge's dominance the USS Halyburton came forward to block the lifeboat's desperate efforts to reach the shore. Using its 15,000 tonne bulk to act as a barrier the lifeboat crashed into the side of it. The anxious pirates were convinced they were going to all be crushed to death as their small stolen craft was pushed out by the monstrous vessel that towered above them.

Enduring this barrage of enforced tactics for 20 minutes the pirates backed off and the intended results paid off. The Navy could claim victory…for now. Within moments, the Navy received a response. The front hatch of the lifeboat opened slowly and a pirate appeared. Having backed away from the mainland the Americans were expecting a submission from the Somalis. But, just seconds after emerging from the waist-up the pirate brandished an AK-47. The pirate aimed it directly at the USS Halyburton and began rapidly firing. Hatred in the pirate's eyes and a snarl strewn across his contorted mouth fuelled the man. As the rat-a-tat-tat of bullets were sprayed at the warship the crew on board cried out into their radios that shots had been fired, alerting their comrades in the other warships.

The pirate didn't cease and continued to maniacally squeeze the trigger of his weapon, a white flash appearing before him as the barrel of his gun burst. Fortunately for the crew on board, no one was hit by the bullets. This did nothing to deter the pirate though, who was quite clearly vexed by the tactics carried out by the Americans and frustrated that they, the pirates, were failing with the operation of their own plan.

The ship didn't return fire and instead chose to wait until the pirate tired and stopped shooting. When he did so, he shot the crew on board a fearless look before submerging himself back into the lifeboat. The look told the men on board the warship that the pirates admitted defeat in knowing that they wouldn't make it to the mainland. But his actions prior to that indicated that they would not submit themselves without fighting to the death.

#   #   #

The night passed and when morning came it told the men on the Indian Ocean that it was Easter Sunday. It was a day usually reserved for peace and prayer. At 5:30 am the pirates, along with their hostage, had been stranded in the lifeboat for 83 hours. The Navy was fully aware that by now the lifeboat was running low on fuel. And with this they knew that so too would the pirates' options be dwindling.

This assumption was affirmed when the pirates radioed in to the USS Bainbridge. Commander Castellano listened attentively. Their message was crystal clear – they needed food and water. The request was like an open door to the Navy's trained hostage negotiators, and they duly seized the moment by stepping in. Naturally concerned for the welfare of Captain Phillips the Navy knew they could act upon the desperation shown by the men and work on it to their advantage. It was all just a matter of time. And biding their time was just one factor the negotiators were skilled in most.

Firstly, they needed to gather information and collect intelligence, which they were certain about obtaining. The pirates were now in a vulnerable position. Not long after making their demands, the pirates were provided with a supply of food and fresh water. After the hungry four men and Captain Phillips had ravenously indulged, the Navy SEALS received yet another unexpected request.

The leader of the pirates asked the commander if he could come aboard the USS Bainbridge. The commander's eyes widened with surprise. The pirate's injury had not been treated properly. It was infected. The negotiators realised that this was an even better scenario than they had hoped for because they would be able to acquire the information they sought much faster while the pirate received the medical care he needed. By splitting up the group and having the leader – subdued and on his own – the crew was aware that they would have the upper hand over him. A quiet confidence settled over the men as Commander Castellano accepted the pirate's request.

With their confidence came an air of caution, however. The Navy knew that the other three pirates would be looking out through the window of their lifeboat to watch what would be going on. Seeing their leader on the deck of the Bainbridge drinking water and generally being well treated by the Americans was sure to create uncertainty among them. In their desperate condition paranoia could easily settle in. What is he telling them? Is he going to give us up? Why are they providing him with more food and water? The Bainbridge relayed these questions to one another because they were all possible questions the pirates could very well be asking themselves and each other.

Once the lead pirate was hauled up to the Bainbridge, watched on suspiciously by the other pirates, he received immediate care to the infected wound on his hand. The negotiators wasted no time in posing questions to him through a translator.

He responded to everything. The ship's crew learned that the pirates were running low on khat – an amphetamine-like drug that is very prevalent in Somalia. The pirates were dependent on this drug as it relieved seasickness. The main problem they were facing, however, was that the gas was running low in the lifeboat. Without enough fuel to get them back to Somalia – and with the warships standing in their way anyway, – and with the lack of khat the pirates were all beginning to suffer with symptoms of seasickness.

Knowing that he and his men were at the mercy of the Navy the pirate set out to seek assurance from them. This was the moment the negotiators had been waiting for and it had come sooner than they had envisaged.

A deal was quickly laid out on the table: the warships would provide the pirates with the security they needed in getting back to the mainland if the Americans were able to tow the pirates there. The negotiators knew that the man would have no hope in altering the deal; he was helplessly in their hands. With no choice whatsoever the pirate silently nodded his consent.

#   #   #

Ninety-four hours aboard the lifeboat and with the deal in place the winch from the USS Bainbridge was attached to the small craft. As soon as the winch was secured the Navy had the lifeboat under their full control. The pirates were under the impression that they were going to be hauled back to Somalia. The Navy, however, had other ideas. They had concocted a plan – a trap – and they set it into motion.

While the lifeboat was being towed along with the three remaining pirates on board the Navy carefully positioned three SEAL snipers on the fan tail of the warship. When the snipers were locked and ready in their designated positions the winch began to gently reel in the lifeboat so it moved closer to the Bainbridge. The pirates were completely oblivious to what was about to happen, while the snipers focused on their nearing targets. With the seasickness taking its toll on them the pirates didn't even notice that they were just 75 feet away from the warship, thus putting them within range for the snipers to make a clean shot.

With the seasickness and restlessness settled among the pirates the crew aboard the Bainbridge noticed that the men had become increasingly agitated. As their frustration escalated rapidly they became aggressive towards each other. Out of nowhere, one of the pirates snatched up his AK-47. The snipers kept their cool and their fingers poised on the trigger of their weapon. They, like the rest of the crew, were aware that this aggressive and unpredictable behaviour from the pirates was jeopardising the life of the captain. All the snipers needed was the signal to fire.

President Obama had sanctioned the Navy and Commander Castellano with the authority to disable the pirates if at any moment they felt that the captain's life was in imminent danger. By now the other pirates had grabbed hold of their deadly weapons and the volume of their aggressive arguing had increased. The threat was clear, so the snipers were issued their orders: kill the pirates, save the captain.

#   #   #

The snipers knew that they had to choreograph their shots simultaneously in order to take down all three pirates at once. Although they were aware of this the shots would be far from easy to execute, being as they were positioned on a moving ship and their intended targets were aboard a bobbing lifeboat on the sea. Despite this though, they had to obey their orders and take the shot. And they only had the one chance to get it right. That one chance had to be the head shot.

Captain Phillips remained seated on the boat. He'd been in the same spot for four days. Unbeknownst to him he'd made the targets slightly easier to the snipers. The snipers had no qualms about potentially hitting him. Through the cab window the snipers locked onto the heads of two of the pirates. The positioning of the third pirate was not so clear. The sniper assigned to him couldn't lock on for the head shot. Because of this, the sniper had to wait to get a clear visual. The snipers understood this. Commander Castellano understood this. The Navy understood this. The American government understood this. The Navy SEAL snipers were trained to only take the shot of his target when in clear view. As soon as he got that clear visual, he and his brothers in arms would each pull the trigger.

Seasickness took its toll on the third pirate eventually. Dizzily, he got to his feet. He needed to fill his lungs with fresh air. He had to escape the stifling humidity. He had to get away from the claustrophobic atmosphere of the lifeboat. He stuck his head out of the window and drew a breath. It would be the last he ever took.

With a clear view the third sniper locked onto his target and relayed the information to the other two. In perfect synchronisation they each fired and after 96 hours the ordeal was over in split seconds as the three pirates all dropped down, instantly dead.

With the mission completed successfully the Navy wasted no time in swooping into action to get Captain Phillips back amongst them. And back home to his loved ones.

Chapter 7: The Trial

Abdulwali Abdukhadir Muse – the name of the lone surviving pirate. He was subsequently arrested and taken to the United States. A fortnight passed after the hijacking and rescue mission. It was a bleak Monday night in New York City. Heavy torrential rain battered the streets. Muse arrived to a packed court under the surveillance of several federal agents. It was like he was a Major League Soccer player being unveiled to a sold out stadium on his debut. Or perhaps it was like he was a 'freak' in a circus show?

Muse, while handcuffed, passed the reporters outside thrusting microphones and questions at him. White lights flashed in his face from the cameras of the photographers. Inside the court room he stood before the judge and jury on prosecution of a federal law that had not been used in the United States of America in decades. To everyone's surprise Muse was not the menacing villain they were expecting. Instead, he was just a tall, thin young man with a boyish friendly face. It was hard to pair his convictions with his appearance. His convictions carried a heavy burden. Muse was facing a mandatory life sentence imprisonment.

The first thing Judge Andrew J. Peck needed to determine was the convict's age. During proceedings Muse remained silent and solemn. He only spoke, through a Somali interpreter, when he was questioned. And even then his answers were quiet and succinct. When Muse claimed he was just a minor, Judge Peck was not convinced.

Deirdre von Dornum, one of Muse's defence lawyers, was keen to present to the court the importance of having the knowledge of this information. It would prove the difference in him being treated as a juvenile and an adult, she explained to the court. This knowledge would determine what kind of facility he would be held in, whether he would be eligible for contact with his family, and how long his sentence would be for.

Muse sat silently in a large chair. It dwarfed his thin appearance. He looked even younger and more helpless. Judge Peck and the lawyers spent more than an hour attempting to figure out just how old he was. During that time Muse sat blocking out the alien tongues around him. He stared at his left hand, still bandaged from the injury he sustained. The wound would turn into a scar that would remind him of the incident for the remainder of his life. The scar held the memory of his three fellow Somali pirates whom he considered friends. Lost friends.

Growing restless of the objections from prosecutors and reporters who were gathered in the courtroom Judge Peck decided to evacuate them all so he could communicate with Muse's father who they were able to contact in Gaalkacyo, Somalia via telephone. With the aid of an interpreter the father – who gave his name as Abdulkadir Muse Ghedi and the information that he was divorced from his son's mother – testified that his son was just a minor in that he was only 15 years of age. His son's date of birth was November 20, 1993. Seizing the moment and for the love of his criminal son Muse Ghedi pleaded to Judge Peck that his family had lived a very simple and traditional nomadic lifestyle, akin to that of millions in Somalia. The father had moved his family around several times throughout his son's upbringing as they followed the pastureland. Despite a few lessons in the Koran for religious purposes, the father revealed that his son was completely uneducated.

Muse Ghedi laid complete blame upon the pirates that had been shot dead by the Navy SEAL snipers. They had tricked his son into joining them in their criminal lives.

With this information the judge and those present in court proceeded with the case.

#   #   #

Proceedings came to a halt. Frederick Galloway
– a rugged New York police detective – came
forward with important new information. He
had just returned from Africa. He'd travelled to
the continent with an investigative team. While
there Detective Galloway had met with Muse's
father. Under the Detective's questioning Muse's
father confessed that he'd lied to the court and to
Judge Peck. Muse Ghedi was a guilty man. He
admitted that he had provided false information
in order to protect his son. Muse's father
revealed that his son was in fact between the age
of 18 and 19.

The court was shocked. Judge Peck was
furious albeit grateful. The judge contacted
Muse's father for a second time. The Somali was
apologetic. Saddened. Hurt. Remorseful. He
confirmed that the news supplied by the
detective was true. Although he was merely
trying to protect his son, in the eyes of God he
knew that lying was wrong. For this he was
seeking his own redemption. Judge Peck
labelled Muse Ghedi's claims as incredibly
deceitful. Shame was laid upon the sunken
shoulders of the man.

Muse was declared as an adult. And so he was prosecuted as one. The crime of piracy was thrown against him. On top of that, Muse was hit with five counts and as a result he was held without bail.

#   #   #

Prosecutors leapt on Muse. He was far from the misguided innocent that his father had painted him out to be, they claimed. He was the leader of this pirate gang. With the veil of privacy afforded to juveniles lifted the hearing was made public.

Prosecutors said that Muse was the first to climb aboard the Maersk Alabama on that fateful morning of April 8, 2009. They revealed that Muse had fired his gun at Captain Phillips when he was spotted on the bridge. They went on to state that that Muse had led two of the armed pirates to the bridge, screaming for money as he did so.

The charges brought against Muse, as well as piracy under the law of nations, included conspiracy to seize a ship by force, conspiracy to commit hostage-taking, and firearms-related charges.

On February 16, 2011 Muse pleaded guilty to his crimes and was sentenced by Judge Peck to spend 33 years and nine months in prison.

Chapter 8: The Aftermath

Three corpses. Corpses of the executed pirates. Executed pirates that were returned to Somalia by the U.S. Navy. Despite this other Somali pirates operating from the same area of the Indian Ocean retaliated angrily and vowed to seek revenge for the deaths of the three. Abdi Garad – portly, rich and notorious Somali pirate commander. He had grown wealthy and fat off the ransom money paid out to his piracy. Ensuring that he continued his role in Somali piracy Garad aggressively voiced his threatening statement of intent. Situated in the Somali port of Harardhere, Garad made a public vow via Al Jazeera that any Americans who were located within the vicinity would be captured and slaughtered like animals. His words did not fall on deaf ears.

Days later a ship bearing the American flag was targeted and rocket-propelled grenades rained down upon it.

From this backlash fears grew over the safety of the 230 foreign sailors aboard more than a dozen ships who were still held captive off the coast of Somalia. Experts were quick to point out that out of every single hijacking that had taken place over the years on a near daily basis off the coast of Somalia only a single hostage had been killed under Somali pirate captivity; the sailor on the Taiwanese fishing ship, Ching Fong Hwa No. 168. The French hostage that was killed during the rescue mission had lost his life accidentally by the rescuers. Experts went as far as to divulge that where the hostages were held the pirates had often reserved a piece of their land for them where they grew food especially for the foreign captives. This, to them, demonstrated that the Somali pirates were not as merciless as was first painted out in the media

Another strike was carried out days afterwards. This time though – to the surprise of many – the attack came on land. Mortar shells were fired at the airport in Mogadishu at the time when US congressman Donald Payne was inside as he was due to leave Somalia. News reports confirmed that there were no casualties.

Garad, who had amassed a fortune estimated to be around $30 million and led a very luxurious life with his three wives, sneered at the news and remained confident that it would only be a matter of time before Americans lost their lives at sea as the Somali pirates, now bloodthirsty and angry, operated in six million square kilometres of ocean sea.

#   #   #

The Maersk Alabama was back sailing the same seas just months after being hijacked. The calls for revenge made by Garad did not go unnoticed with pirates in the area though. They paid heed to his lethal words.

On November 18, 2009 the Maersk Alabama sailed some 350 nautical miles past the east side of Somalia. It was bright and early in the morning, but the pirates had been out all night just waiting for their opportunity to seize upon a foreign vessel. When they spotted the infamous American cargo ship they could not believe their luck. A gang of four pirates in a skiff drew their automatic rifles and opened fire. The ship was now well guarded, however, and the security aboard immediately leaped into action by firing back. The pirates fled realising they could not succeed.

The crew aboard the ship had been quick to send an alert out as well and not long after the incident had occurred, a patrol plane based in Djibouti was at the scene along with an EU ship, which helped search the area for the pirates. Their search proved unsuccessful though. The pirates had got away.

Nearly a year later, on September 29, 2010, the Maersk Alabama was once again targeted by pirates off the east coast of Somalia. This time, five pirates in a skiff fired their AK-47's but the security on the ship was able to repel the attack by doing their job in defending the vessel.

The same thing happened on March 8, 2011 when news confirmed that a third attempt had been made. It was a repeat of the previous two incidents – pirates in a travelling skiff fired their automatic weapons in the direction of the American vessel, which was saved by the security on board. As before, the pirates were forced to turn away.

Two months later though, May 14, the Maersk Alabama received its biggest scare when the pirates got closer than they had done in previous attempts. It was around midnight. The ship was travelling westbound in the night. Out of nowhere they realised in the dark that five pirates had silently approached in a skiff. They had altered their tactics this time and ceasing their fire they managed to close in to 30 metres of the ship. It was when they were preparing a hook ladder to climb aboard that the Maersk Alabama's security team noticed the gang below. Two quick shots were fired into the skiff. The pirates knew they had failed once again. They broke away and escaped. They couldn't rue the missed opportunity too much though. Instead they realised that the Maersk Alabama was not completely untouchable.

#   #   #

Back in the United States the Maersk Alabama crew returned home safely to a national hero's welcome. Many of those featured in the news appeared in interviews where they recounted details of their ship's hijacking and the rescue mission that ensued. Though the majority were positive in their interviews some were bitter about the events that put their lives at risk. One of those men was Chief Engineer Mike Perry.

The messages that Captain Phillips had received in the days that led to the hijacking were revealed in the news. Seven. There had been seven warning messages. Seven warning messages had haunted the captain's mind, and now they had returned to haunt him.

The news revealed that the messages came from maritime safety groups. Dangers lay ahead, they said. Pirates. That word.

An alternative route had been planned. It would have come at the expense of an extra day added to their journey time. Captain Phillips had chosen to ignore these though. As a result, his band of brothers disbanded and some turned against him. The captain was lambasted by them publicly for having ignored the warnings and thus putting their lives in danger. Chief Engineer Perry in particular, who had demonstrated such heroics, was enraged by the revelations.

Chief Engineer Perry received the backing of the ship's navigator and helmsman. A fourth member was Chief Steward Richard E. Hicks. He was so distraught and angered by the event that at the end of April in 2009 he filed a lawsuit against his employer, Waterman Steamship Corporation and Maersk Line Ltd.

Hicks' Houston attorney explained that his client had had to endure nearly 12 hours in a cramped engine room with no light, food or enough liquids in temperatures as high as 130 degrees. All along his employers and the captain had been fully aware of the dangers that faced the crew. They were blamed for unnecessarily exposing their employees to the imminent danger. Despite this, they had not acquired a level of security. Hicks claimed he was still suffering from physical injuries he sustained as well as from the trauma of the incident, which put him in fear of returning to his job.

After Hicks filed his lawsuit 10 other members of the crew came forward. Each had their own lawsuit. There were claims of bodily injuries and insufficient compensation paid out by their employers. As they continued to pile up Waterman Steamship Corporation and Maersk Line Ltd were looking at a total almost reaching $50 million in damages.

Though more than half of the crew ended up turning against Captain Phillips and the ship's owners there were those who retained their loyalty. One of them was Captain Shane Murphy, Captain Phillips' second-in-command. He publicly fledged his support, much to the chagrin of his former colleagues.

\#   \#   \#

Despite the saga of the other crew members Captain Richard Phillips received very positive coverage in the media. President Barack Obama was the first to lead the praise of the bravery demonstrated by Captain Phillips during the ordeal and the mission that followed. The President, full of high esteem, told the nation that the captain was a role model for Americans. The captain's courage and selfless concern for the welfare of his crew was something to admire. It was food for thought for the people of America.

   On May 9, 2009 – a little over a month after the hijacking of the Maersk Alabama had made global news – Captain Phillips and his wife, Andrea Coggio, were invited to the Oval Office where they met President Obama.

Later that year Captain Phillips had a book published about his story. The book, titled *A Captain's Duty*, had the rights bought the same year by Columbia Pictures. No sooner had the book hit the shelves than a script for the film was put together by Billy Ray, the scriptwriter behind movies such as *State of Play* and *The Hunger Games*. A production team was assembled for the Maersk Alabama film. They included Scott Rudin, Michael DeLuca, Kevin Spacey and Dana Brunetti – the same production team who worked on *The Social Network*. Tom Hanks, Academy Award winner for *Philadelphia* and *Forrest Gump*, was given the lead role in the film. Unsurprisingly, the movie is called *Captain Phillips*.

#   #   #

Commander Frank Castellano was highly praised for the action he took in saving the life of Captain Phillips. He realised that the captain's life was in imminent danger during the rescue mission. He recognised the threat of the growing agitation demonstrated by the three pirates on board the lifeboat. Commander Castellano recalled the standing orders assigned to him by President Obama whereby he was to take the necessary actions in ensuring the captain survived the rescue mission. For his exemplary leadership qualities Commander Castellano was awarded the Meritorious Service Medal, the Navy and Marine Corps Commendation Medal, and the Navy Surface Warfare Badge.

#   #   #

The five-ton lifeboat, pot-marked with bullet holes, was donated to the National Navy UDT-Seal Museum in Fort Pierce, Florida in August 2009. It remains on display there, alongside a Mark 11 Mod 0 (SR-25) sniper rifle – the same one used by the Navy SEAL snipers.

Epilogue

President Obama stepped forward. He had a speech to make. The gathered audience waited. They watched him. He seemed to eye each one of them individually. Though no one spoke questions were raised. So what lay ahead? How could piracy be prevented? How could the 2,000 miles of coast line by Somalia continue as one of the busiest shipping lanes in the world?

The President looked down at his papers and gathered his thoughts. Europe and the United States were heavily reliant on the access to this route. As they had increased their international transferring of trade goods so too had Somalia with their pirates. They, like the traders, had families to provide for. Their country was at war with itself. What choices did they have available to them? They were desperate. Matters had to be taken into their own hands. The weak institutions in their nation had cracked open a window of lawless opportunity. Through it, they could see international riches. Taunting them. Mocking their misery. Daily. And so it was that these taunts were turned into salvation and survival.

The cameras were trained on the President who remained silent. There was an overwhelming increase in the number of reported pirate hijackings in a two-year period. Ransoms had been paid. The corruption had made the Somalis grow richer. With the money came greed, boldness and inevitably, more pirates.

In the crowd President Obama picked out Commander Castellano. They locked eye contact for a moment. Knowing that something needed to be done before the situation escalated and more lives were lost, especially after the Maersk Alabama hijacking was made infamous by the gripping globalisation of its news coverage in the media, the United States and President Obama led the international community in the battle against modern piracy. The combat took time and patience. However, figures revealed genuine progress had been achieved. Pirates had 31 foreign vessels and 710 foreign hostages in their captivity. One year later, since the fight against them had been initiated, the pirates had just eight foreign vessels in captivity along with 213 hostages. This was almost a 70 per cent decline.

Commander Castellano gave a resolute nod to the President. The President's eyes scanned once more and fell upon Captain Phillips, who sat beside his wife. Their hands were locked. Their faces displayed pride. They were all here to learn how the figures added up. How had success been achieved?

The huge difference demonstrated that the strategy undertaken by President Obama and his administration had been executed with a precision that had effectively achieved results on a huge scale in rapid time. The crowd waited to hear what steps had been taken in making such significant progress:

For one, a diplomatic engagement was made in order to galvanise a united international action; extra security measures had been carried out on the troubled waters with additional support provided for private vessels through the use of naval assets, which could prevent pirate attacks; encouragement had been shown to industries to protect themselves in order to disrupt pirate hijackings; the use of strong legal prosecution and heavy punishment were made effective as a deterrence; and the networks that aided pirates in their missions were debilitated.

Furthermore, the United States had established the Contact Group on Piracy off the Coast of Somalia, which drew in support from countries around the world in order to prompt action and rid the world of modern piracy. More than 70 nations had pledged their support.

This was what the people wanted to hear. This was what the President was going to tell them. President Obama narrowed his eyes, opened his mouth, and began his speech.

References

Archer, Venetia and Young Pelton, Robert. *Can We Ever Assess the True Cost of Piracy?* Somalia Report. February 21, 2012. Report.

Associated Press. *Pirates Hijack Two Tankers Within 24 Hours Off Somali Shore.* March 26, 2009. Fox News. Report.
http://www.foxnews.com/story/0,2933,510766,00 .html

Axe, David. *Somalia Redux: a more hands off approach.* 2009. Report.

BBC Wales. *Sir Henry Morgan.* 2009.
www.bbc.co.uk/wales/southeast/halloffame/his torical_figures/henry_morgan.shtml

BBC History. *Vikings*
www.bbc.co.uk/history/ancient/vikings

BBC News. *FBI in hostage talks with Somalis.* April 9, 2009. Report.
http://news.bbc.co.uk/1/hi/world/africa/7991114. stm

BBC News. *Somali pirate sentenced to 33 years in US prison*. February 16, 2011. Report. **http://www.bbc.co.uk/news/world-us-canada-12486129**

BBC News. *Seized tanker anchors off Somalia*. November 19, 2008. Report. **http://news.bbc.co.uk/1/hi/world/africa/7735507.stm**

BBC News. *US crew seized by Somali pirates*. April 8, 2009. Report. **http://news.bbc.co.uk/1/hi/world/africa/7989474.stm**

Bryant, Terry. *Maersk Alabama Crew Member Files Lawsuit against Employer for Failing to Protect Him from Pirates*. Houston, Texas. April 27, 2009. Press Release. **http://www.terrybryant.com/pdf/BTB%20Maersk%20Line%20Press%20Release.pdf**

Classis Britannica **www.classis-britannica.co.uk/sml/index.htm**

CNN. *Crewman's e-mail gives harrowing details of hijacking*. April 20, 2009. Report. **http://edition.cnn.com/2009/WORLD/africa/04/16/somalia.hijacked.ship.email/index.html**

CNN. *U.S. negotiators try to persuade pirates to free captain*. April 10, 2009. Report. **http://edition.cnn.com/2009/WORLD/africa/04/0 9/ship.hijacked/index.html**

Cowell, Alan. *Pirates Attack Maersk Alabama Again*. New York Times. November 18, 2009. Report. **http://www.nytimes.com/2009/11/19/world/afric a/19pirates.html?_r=0**

Dagne, Ted. *Somalia: Conditions and Prospects for Lasting Peace*. Congressional Research Service. August 31, 2011. Report.

Fitzpatrick, David. *Pirates set sights on Maersk Alabama again, maritime group says*. CNN. November 22, 2010. Report. **http://articles.cnn.com/2010-11- 22/world/maersk.alabama.targeted.again_1_ma ersk-alabama-somali-pirates-somali- coast?_s=PM:WORLD**

Guardian News. *Teenage Somali pirate arrives in US facing trial over Maersk Alabama attack*. April 21, 2009. Report. **http://www.guardian.co.uk/world/2009/apr/21/s omali-pirate-maersk-alabama-richard-phillips**

Kit, Borys. *Tom Hanks to Play Capt. Richard Phillips in Somali Pirate Hostage Story.* March 15, 2011. The Hollywood Reporter. **http://www.hollywoodreporter.com/news/tom-hanks-play-capt-richard-167846**

Maersk A-Class. Global Security. April 9, 2009. **http://www.globalsecurity.org/military/systems/ship/maersk-a.htm**

Maliti, Tom, Muhumed, Malkhadir, and Hassan, Mohamed Olad. *Somali pirates a far cry from buccaneers of old.* Washington. Washington Times. December 17, 2011. Report.

Mertens, Jan. *Shipping Companies (Denmark).* Copenhagen. CRW Flags. December 11, 2003. **http://www.crwflags.com/fotw/flags/dk~hfa.html#apmol**

Miriri, Duncan. *Somali pirates killed Chinese sailor-official.* Reuters. November 15, 2007. **http://www.reuters.com/article/2007/11/15/idUSL15534801**

Mitropoulos, Efthimios E. *Piracy: orchestrating the response.* International Maritime Organization. February 3, 2011. Report.

Reinhart, John. *Maersk Alabama fact sheet.*
December 4, 2009. Press release
**http://www.maersk.com/Press/NewsAndPressR
eleases/Pages/APMM080409.aspx**

Sky News. *Pirates Issue New Threat Over US
Hostage.* April 11, 2009. Report.
**http://news.sky.com/story/684829/pirates-issue-
new-threat-over-us-hostage**

The Advantage of Piracy. Berlin. German Foreign
Policy. September 9, 2010. **http://www.german-
foreign-policy.com/en/fulltext/57866**

Treadway, Tyler. *Bullet-marked lifeboat from pirate
kidnapping arrives to applause at new home at SEAL
museum in Fort Pierce.* TCPalm. August 14, 2009.
Report.
**http://www.tcpalm.com/news/2009/aug/14/bulle
t-marked-lifeboat-pirate-kidnapping-arrives-a/**

Tristam, Pierre. *Barbary Pirates.* About.com.
middleeast.about.com/od/b/g/Barbary-pirates-
glossary.htm

Weiser, Benjamin. *Pirate Suspect Charged as Adult
in New York.* The New York Times. April 21,
2009. Report.
**http://www.nytimes.com/2009/04/22/nyregion/2
2pirate.html?_r=2&hp**

YouTube. *The Real Maersk Alabama/Somali Pirate Story*. June 22, 2009. Film.
http://www.youtube.com/watch?v=rMvGIqa-ZlM

Printed in Great Britain
by Amazon

64900439R00047